SUPER SIMPLE

EARTH DAY

ACTIVITIES

❧ FUN AND EASY HOLIDAY PROJECTS FOR KIDS ❧

Megan Borgert-Spaniol

Consulting Editor, Diane Craig, M.A./Reading Specialist

Super Sandcastle

An Imprint of Abdo Publishing
abdopublishing.com

abdopublishing.com

Published by Abdo Publishing, a division of ABDO, PO Box 398166, Minneapolis, Minnesota 55439.
Copyright © 2018 by Abdo Consulting Group, Inc. International copyrights reserved in all countries.
No part of this book may be reproduced in any form without written permission from the publisher.
Super SandCastle™ is a trademark and logo of Abdo Publishing.

Printed in the United States of America, North Mankato, Minnesota

102017
012018

THIS BOOK CONTAINS
RECYCLED MATERIALS

Design: Alison Stuerman, Mighty Media, Inc.
Production: Mighty Media, Inc.
Editor: Rebecca Felix
Cover Photographs: Mighty Media, Inc.; Shutterstock
Interior Photographs: iStockphoto; Mighty Media, Inc.; Shutterstock

The following manufacturers/names appearing in this book are trademarks: Aero®, Burpee®,
Craft Smart®, Crunch®, Elmer's® Glue-All™, M&M'S®, Mars®, Oreo®, Sharpie®, Sharpwriter®

Publisher's Cataloging-in-Publication Data

Names: Borgert-Spaniol, Megan, author.
Title: Super simple Earth Day activities: fun and easy holiday projects for kids /
by Megan Borgert-Spaniol.
Other titles: Fun and easy holiday projects for kids
Description: Minneapolis, Minnesota : Abdo Publishing, 2018. | Series: Super simple holidays |
Identifiers: LCCN 2017946524 | ISBN 9781532112447 (lib.bdg.) | ISBN 9781614799863 (ebook)
Subjects: LCSH: Earth Day--Juvenile literature. | Handicraft--Juvenile literature. |
    Holiday decorations--Juvenile literature.
Classification: DDC 745.594162--dc23
LC record available at https://lccn.loc.gov/2017946524

Super SandCastle™ books are created by a team of professional educators, reading specialists,
and content developers around five essential components—phonemic awareness, phonics,
vocabulary, text comprehension, and fluency—to assist young readers as they develop reading
skills and strategies and increase their general knowledge. All books are written, reviewed,
and leveled for guided reading and early reading intervention for use in shared, guided, and
independent reading and writing activities to support a balanced approach to literacy instruction.

TO ADULT HELPERS

The craft projects in this series are fun and simple. There are just a few things to remember to keep kids safe. Some projects require the use of sharp or hot objects or involve food items with allergy triggers. Also, kids may be using messy materials such as glue or paint. Make sure they protect their clothes and work surfaces. Review the projects before starting and be ready to assist when necessary.

KEY SYMBOLS

Watch for these warning symbols in this book. Here is what each one means.

HOT!
This project requires the use of a hot tool. Get help!

NUTS!
This project includes the use of nuts. Make sure no one handling it has a nut allergy.

SHARP!
You will be working with a sharp object. Get help!

CONTENTS

HAPPY HOLIDAYS!

Holidays are great times to celebrate with family and friends. Many people have favorite holiday **traditions**. Some traditions are hundreds of years old. But people start new traditions too, such as making holiday foods and crafts.

EARTH DAY

The first Earth Day took place on April 22, 1970, in the United States. This is when the US government began efforts to protect Earth's air, water, and land.

Earth Day celebrates this protection. It raises awareness about the **environment**. Today, more than one **billion** people around the world take part in this holiday.

CELEBRATE EARTH DAY

Earth Day is a global holiday. People across the world celebrate it in many ways. How do you celebrate Earth Day?

ASSEMBLE

Millions of people join marches and **rallies** on Earth Day. They watch holiday parades. They gather in public to show how important it is to protect the **environment**.

VOLUNTEER

People **volunteer** on Earth Day. Many pick up trash from parks and riverbeds. Others plant trees. These small actions add up to make a big difference.

REDUCE, REUSE, RECYCLE

Throughout the year, people reduce, reuse, and recycle. They reduce use of electricity. They reuse clothing or other items. And they recycle plastic, paper, and more. On Earth Day, many people **inform** others why these actions are important.

MATERIALS

Here are some of the materials that you will need for the projects in this book.

ACRYLIC PAINT

AIR-DRY CLAY

BEADS

BIRDSEED

CARD STOCK

CHENILLE STEMS

CHOCOLATE PUDDING CUPS

COLORED PAPER

COLORED TISSUE PAPER

CRAFT GLUE

FLOWER SEEDS

GLITTER

GOOGLY EYES

GUMMY WORMS

HAMMER

HOLE PUNCH

HOT GLUE GUN & GLUE STICKS

JEWELS

LARGE, SMOOTH-SIDED JAR

MARKERS

NAILS

OREO COOKIES

PAINTBRUSHES

PAPER EDGER SCISSORS

PAPER TOWEL TUBES

PEANUT BUTTER

POTTING SOIL

RIBBON

SMALL CONTAINERS WITH LIDS

YARN

GLOBAL GREETING CARD

Craft an artistic planet card to say
"Happy Earth Day!"

WHAT YOU NEED

card stock

marker

small bowl or lid

pencil

green & blue
    tissue paper

scissors

craft glue

paper plate

1 Fold the card stock in half crosswise. Write "Happy Earth Day!" on the front of the folded card stock near the top.

2 Trace the small bowl or lid beneath the writing. This circle represents Earth. Draw lines inside it to outline areas of land.

3 Cut the tissue paper into small squares.

4 Squirt glue on a paper plate. Wrap one square around the eraser end of a pencil. Dip the tissue-covered eraser in glue.

5 Glue the blue tissue squares in the ocean areas inside the circle.

6 Glue the green squares in the land areas. Let the glue dry.

7 Give someone your greeting card to celebrate the holiday!

PLANET GARLAND

Turn recycled paper into a string of planets that resemble Earth!

WHAT YOU NEED

green & blue paper

paper edger scissors

craft glue

small bowl or lid

marker

scissors

yarn

clear tape

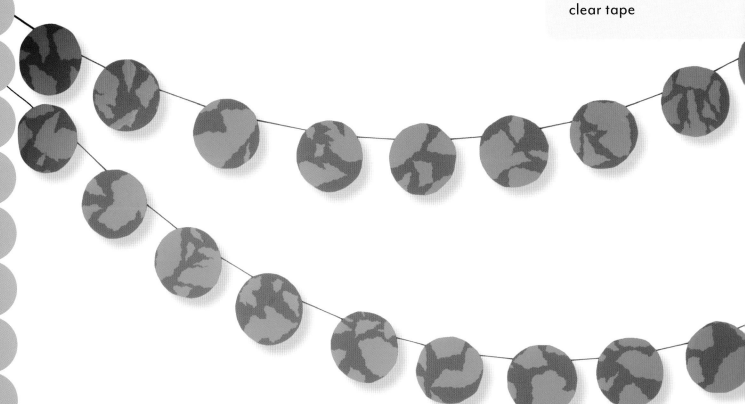

1 Use paper edger scissors to cut shapes out of green paper. These will be the land areas.

2 Glue the green shapes **randomly** onto the blue paper. Let the glue dry.

3 Use a small bowl or lid to trace circles onto the patterned paper. Cut out the circles. Each one represents a planet that looks like Earth.

4 Repeat steps 1 through 3 to make about 20 planets.

5 Lay the planets facedown in a line on a table or floor. Space them evenly.

6 Lay a long piece of yarn across the tops of the planets. Tape the yarn down.

7 Leave extra yarn on both ends for hanging your Earth Day **garland**!

EARTHWORM SNACKS

Make sweet snacks of worms wiggling atop layers of edible earth!

WHAT YOU NEED

8 to 10 Oreo cookies

gallon plastic zippered bag

rolling pin

measuring cups

sweetened shredded coconut

bowl

green food coloring

spoon

4 chocolate pudding cups

gummy worms

1 Place the Oreo cookies in the plastic bag. Seal the bag. Crush the cookies with a rolling pin.

2 Put ½ cup of the coconut into a small bowl. Add six drops of green food coloring. Stir the coconut until it is green.

3 Open a pudding cup. This is the soil. Sprinkle some crushed cookies on top of the pudding. This makes a layer of dirt.

4 Sprinkle some green coconut on top of the crushed cookies. This is the grass.

5 Place gummy worms on top of the grass.

6 Repeat steps 3 through 5 with the other pudding cups.

7 Share your Earth Day treats with friends or family members!

SEED SOUNDS GUESSING GAME

Create a game to see what sounds seeds can make. Plant the seeds after playing!

WHAT YOU NEED

8 to 10 small identical containers with lids

various seeds

paper

marker

scissors

double-sided tape

decorative stickers

16

1 Put the same amount of one type of seed in two of the containers.

2 Repeat step 1 with the other types of seeds. Create at least four pairs of seeds.

3 Cut small strips of paper for the container bottoms. On one strip, write the type of seed that is inside one container. Tape the strip to the bottom of that container. Repeat for all containers.

4 Decorate the containers if you like. But make sure they all look the same!

5 It's time to play! Scramble the containers on a table. Shake each container without looking at the labels. Try to match pairs based on their sounds.

6 Once you have paired up all the containers, read their labels. How many seed sounds did you correctly match?

SPRING GRASS CROWN

Turn paper into a crown of sprouting spring grass!

WHAT YOU NEED

2 sheets of
    green paper

ruler

scissors

tape

decorative stickers
    or markers

18

1 Cut 2 inches (5 cm) off one long side of each sheet of paper.

2 Cut long, narrow triangles into one of the long sides of each piece of paper. The paper should begin to look like grass.

3 Place the two strips of grass end to end. Tape them together at the **seam**.

4 Decorate the grass with stickers or drawings of flowers or insects.

5 Wrap the grass around your head. Have an adult help tape the ends together so the crown fits **snugly**.

6 Wear your crown to celebrate Earth Day!

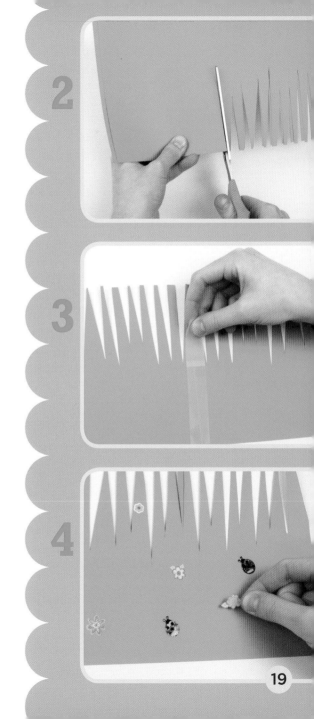

SEED BOMBS

Scatter these seed clusters and wait for flowers to bloom!

WHAT YOU NEED

air-dry clay

large,
    smooth-sided jar

plastic cup

potting soil

packets of
    flower seeds

dinner knife

20

1 Break off a piece of clay that is about as large as your fist. Roll it out using the jar.

2 Fill the cup halfway with potting soil. Spread the soil on top of the clay. Keep the soil in the center, leaving a border of clay.

3 Sprinkle a packet of seeds on top of the soil.

(continued on next page)

TIP You can mix several types of flower seeds together in one seed bomb if you like.

21

4

5

6

4 Fold the clay over the soil. Be careful to avoid spilling any soil or seeds.

5 Slowly work the soil and seeds into the clay. **Knead** the clay, pressing firmly. Continue kneading until there is no more loose soil. Be patient!

6 Use your hands to roll the ball of clay, soil, and seeds into a long log.

7 Cut the log into smaller pieces.

8 Roll the smaller pieces into balls. Let the balls dry in the sun.

9 Your seed bombs are ready to be taken outside! Drop them in your garden and watch them grow. Just be sure to place them where there is soil and sunlight.

TIP Seeds need water to grow. Water the seed bombs you dropped to help them grow.

RE-USE-IT MOBILE

Turn recyclables and unwanted junk into a masterpiece!

- newspaper
- paper towel tube
- toilet paper tubes
- acrylic paint
- paintbrush
- scissors
- craft glue
- recycled items, such as toilet paper tubes & plastic caps, containers & lids
- scrap wooden board
- hammer
- nail
- decorative items, such as jewels, glitter & beads
- yarn or wire
- unwanted junk items, such as old jewelry & keys
- wooden skewer
- string

NOTE

The following steps are suggestions for using the listed materials. You can adjust your steps based on what materials you have!

1 Cover your work surface with newspaper. Paint the paper towel tube and toilet paper tubes. Let the paint dry.

2 Cut the toilet paper tubes into sections. Glue the pieces together to create shapes.

3 Place plastic caps on the wooden board. Use a hammer and nail to make holes in their centers. Decorate the caps.

4 String the items you made onto pieces of yarn or wire. String junk items too. Tie a knot under each item to keep it in place.

5 Tie a long piece of string through the paper towel tube to make a hanger.

6 Push the skewer through the paper towel tube to make a set of holes. Make one set for each **strand**. Thread a strand through one set of holes. Tie a bead to its end above the tube. Repeat for all strands. Then hang your **mobile** for all to see!

SWEET SEED BIRD FEEDER

Make a simple, Earth-friendly treat to feed backyard birds!

WHAT YOU NEED

toilet paper tube

2 wooden skewers

hole punch

ribbon

peanut butter

dinner knife

plate

birdseed

scissors

1 Poke the wooden skewers through the toilet paper tube near one end, as shown. Remove the skewers.

2 Punch one hole on each side of the toilet paper tube on the opposite end from the skewer holes. String a long piece of ribbon through these larger holes. Tie its ends in a knot to make a **loop** for hanging.

3 Spread a thin layer of peanut butter all over the tube.

4 Put birdseed on the plate. Roll the tube in the birdseed.

5 Cut the sharp ends off the skewers. Then poke the skewers back through the holes in the tube. The skewers are perches for the birds.

6 Hang your homemade feeder outside. Watch as birds flock to it!

RECYCLED PAPER PLANET COLLAGE

Revamp scraps of recycled paper into a collage representing Earth!

1 Trace around the bowl on the card stock. The circle represents Earth.

2 Draw land shapes inside the circle.

3 Use various paper punches to cut shapes out of the recycled paper.

4 Glue the green shapes to the land areas on the card stock. Glue the blue shapes to the ocean areas on the card stock.

5 Cut your planet out. Glue it to a piece of the blue paper.

6 Punch or cut out stars from colored paper. Glue them to the sky surrounding the planet.

7 Display your collage on Earth Day!

TIP You can punch shapes out of old magazines! Choose pages with green and blue text or images.

PLASTIC CAP INSECTS

Celebrate some of Earth's smallest creatures by turning plastic caps into bright little bugs!

WHAT YOU NEED

chenille stems

plastic caps

hot glue gun
   & glue sticks

scissors

recycled paper

marker

googly eyes

1 Twist three chenille stems together at their centers.

2 Bend the stems so they fit **snugly** inside the cap. Hot glue the centers of the chenille stems inside the cap. These stems will be the legs. Trim the ends to shorten the legs if you like.

3 Fold a sheet of recycled paper in half. Draw a wing shape at the **crease**. Cut out the shape and unfold the wings.

4 Glue the wings and googly eyes to the top of the cap.

5 Repeat steps 1 through 4 to make more insects.

6 Set your insects out at home on a shelf or windowsill. Or, take them to school to liven up your locker!

GLOSSARY

billion – a very large number. One billion is also written 1,000,000,000.

crease – a sharp line made by folding something.

environment – nature and everything in it, such as the land, sea, and air.

garland – a decorative ring or rope made of leaves, flowers, or some other material.

inform – to tell a person the facts known about an event or subject.

knead – to press, fold, and stretch something, such as bread dough.

loop – a circle made by a rope, string, or thread.

mobile – an artistic device with parts that are arranged so they will move in the air currents.

rally – a large group of people gathered to support or oppose a cause.

randomly – done without any order, purpose, or method.

seam – the line where two edges meet.

snugly – in a way that is very tight or close-fitting.

strand – one of many threads or parts of a thread that make up something larger.

tradition – a belief or practice passed through a family or group of people.

volunteer – to offer to do a job, most often without pay.